chapman

chapmaN

Beautiful Stuff!

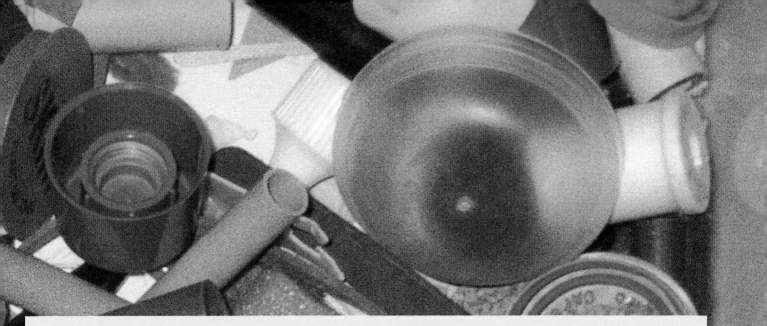

Beautiful Stuff!

Learning with Found Materials

by Cathy Weisman Topal and Lella Gandini

Davis Publications, Inc.
Worcester, Massachusetts

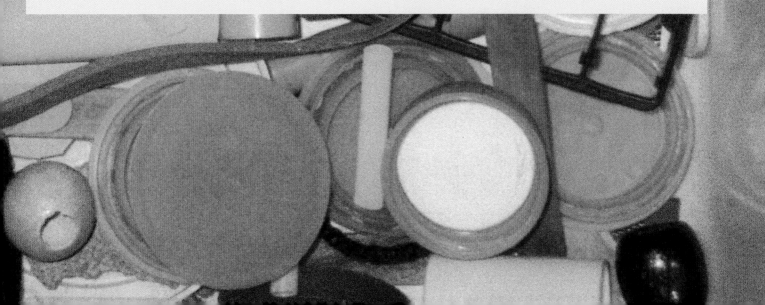

Printed in Italy
Library of Congress Number: 98-87575
ISBN: 0-87192-388-2
10 9 8 7 6 5 4 3 2 1

Publisher: Wyatt Wade

Editorial Director: Claire Mowbray Golding

Production Editors: Laura Marshall Alavosus, Nancy Burnett

Assistant Editor: Mary Ellen Wilson

Manufacturing Coordinator: Jenna Sturgis

Copyeditor: Laura Marshall Alavosus

Design: Janis Owens

We dedicate this book to our children — Simone, Rachel, Claire, Tim, Andrew, Ian, Susan, and Barbara — so that they can play with our grandchildren, Rowen and Sasha and those to come.

Acknowledgements

We would like to thank the educators of Reggio Emilia, Italy, who continue to inspire and challenge us and from whom we have learned so much.

We thank the children, teachers, and parents at the Fort Hill Preschool and the Smith College Campus School for joining with us on this adventure with materials. We especially thank Rita Harris and Debbie Grubbs, Shauneen Kroll, Sue Rudnitsky, Beth Haxby, Barbara Baker, Lois Ducharme, Michelle Dilts, Suzanne Chambers, Janice Henderson, Linda Smith, Laura Taylor, Robin Jurs, and Maureen Litwin for opening their classrooms to us, trying out new materials, and photographing, observing, and recording children's ideas. We also wish to thank Cathy Hoter-Reid for believing in and supporting this project.

We are grateful to the readers of this manuscript whose comments and suggestions helped us clarify our thinking: Pamela Houk, John Nimmo, Dave Kelly, Lynne Brill, Susan Etheredge, and Mary Beth Radke.

Wyatt Wade and Claire Mowbray Golding from Davis Publications, Inc., read many versions of this book over the years and were instrumental in helping us to arrive at this picture essay format.

Finally, we wish to thank our husbands, Sam Topal and Lester Little, for their enthusiastic support and encouragement.

Contents

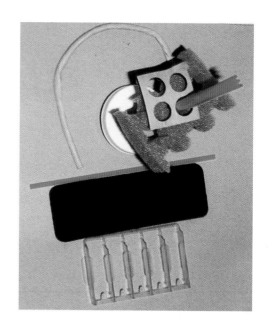

Contents

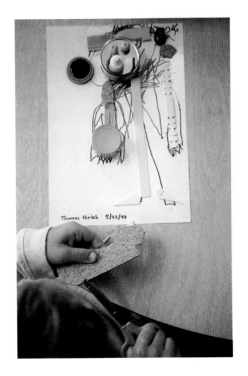

Chapter 5
Extending and Displaying Our Work / 89

Preface

After many requests from educators, we prepared this guide to help teachers and parents foster meaningful experiences between young children and materials. Many of the ways of working and the beliefs discussed in this book have been inspired by educators from Reggio Emilia, Italy, and by the exhibition, "The Hundred Languages of Children." Principles of the Reggio Emilia approach include:

- a deep respect for the ideas of children and teachers.
- a belief that knowledge is constructed through social exchange.
- the value of using materials and media to express and communicate feelings, thoughts, and understandings.
- the desire to document children's and teachers' processes to preserve memories and sustain in-depth work.
- the joy and growth that comes from collaborating with other teachers and with children in the search for knowledge and understanding of relationships.

Our journey with materials took place with a number of teachers from the Fort Hill Preschool and two kindergarten classrooms. Cathy Topal spends two mornings a week in the preschool and kindergarten as a visual arts teacher. Lella Gandini consults with teachers about aspects of the Reggio Emilia approach. Most of the experiences presented here took place with four-year-old children, their parents, and teachers in the classroom of Rita Harris and Debbie Grubbs. We worked with teachers who had the desire to experiment and discover with us. This helped us learn a great deal about

A child uses her self-portrait as a blueprint for representing herself with materials.

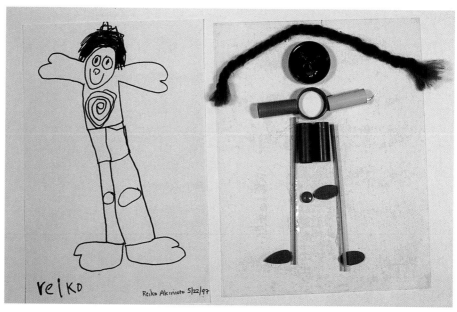

reiko

Reiko Akimoto 5/22/97

daily occurrences, strategies, and ways of setting up and organizing situations for learning.

Rather than focusing on the creation of products, this book is based on observation and recording of children's and teachers' processes. As you turn the pages, you will become a participant in our journey while you construct a way of working with materials that you find appropriate for your situation. We offer you ideas and suggestions that come from real-life experiences in a school.

The participation of parents is as fundamental to gathering materials and generating strong interest as it is to the life of the school.

You will also encounter our moments of doubt. Having doubts, we feel, is part of growing as educators. We know that there are many materials to explore, but we chose to focus on found and recyclable materials because they surround us in the environment. The shapes, colors, and textures in these often-discarded objects can create a bridge to visual and active learning. We watched this process unfold while we worked on this book.

Safety First
Potential Choking Hazard

Please use great care and good judgment when collecting and using materials with young children. Teachers, parents, and other adults should carefully determine that the materials they are using are clean and not sharp, toxic, or potentially harmful before allowing young children to use them. These activities, as do all activities that involve young children, require close and uninterrupted adult supervision. The activities in this book are appropriate for children who are four years of age and older. Be sure to keep small items away from very young children. Children under the age of three or four often put small objects in their mouths, creating a potential choking harzard.
The authors and publisher cannot be held responsible for any misuses of materials by children or adults.

Introduction

Children explore materials by first noticing, then touching them.

To a young child, the world is full of materials to touch, discover, and explore. To find, collect, sort, and use materials is to embark on a special kind of adventure. For adults, gathering materials means rediscovering the richness and beauty in natural, unexpected, and recyclable objects that are all around us, but not often noticed.

One way to rediscover our own creative impulses is to see possibilities in materials. Children possess a natural openness to the potential of materials. When adults become aware of this process, they find ways to watch and listen to children. Children and adults become collaborators as they discover, collect, sort, arrange, experiment, create, construct, and think with materials. The goal is to allow children to become fluent with materials—as if materials were a language.

Sharing is an important part of the experience.

I look. I search. I hope to see
something that appeals to me.
Something unique — or maybe not.
Buttons, milk caps, straws — the lot.
A blue-green shape just caught my eye.
I don't think I can pass it by.
Whatever it is, it makes me glad.
And so, I'll put it in my bag!

—Rita Harris, teacher

(Above) A collection reveals small treasures.

(Opposite) Organizing items helps us see what we've collected.

Collecting, Discovering, and Organizing Materials

Chapter 1

Collecting, Discovering, and Organizing Materials

*O*ver the last few years, we have encouraged the teachers and parents in our school to collect interesting materials, and find effective ways of using them. As materials come into the classroom, simple bottle caps, broken jewelry, extruded objects, and scraps of paper and cardboard are transformed into treasures. In studying how materials can fuel ideas and thinking, we realize that it is the noticing and gathering of the materials that initially sparks our interest, enthusiasm, and awareness. We decide it is crucial to involve children and parents in the process of collecting.

Getting Started

To begin this investigation, we need to prepare parents for their children's requests for materials. Together, we write the following letter:

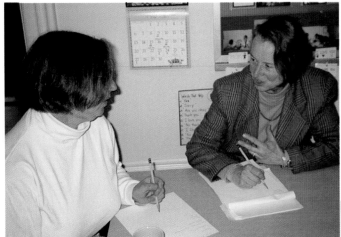

Rita and Lella share their thoughts and ideas, and plan for the first meeting with children. Cathy takes these photographs to record the beginning of this adventure.

Collecting, Discovering, and Organizing Materials

Dear Parents,

We would like to investigate what it means to children when they have sought out, discovered, and collected materials themselves. Does this affect the way they use and care for those materials? Are they more thoughtful, focused, and pleased with their efforts when they have been engaged in the process right from the beginning?

Today you will get a letter from your child asking you to help him or her look for potentially useful materials to bring to school to enrich the studio area in our classroom. We hope you will like scouting out the treasures that you have around your house. We are very interested in any perceptions that you or your child has about this process. Any interesting dialogue or quotes about materials that you can record would be helpful, too. Please let us know your thoughts.

Sincerely,
Group A Teachers

P.S. Please make sure that materials are clean!

Teachers begin collecting clear and white containers for sorting and distributing materials. Clear or white containers showcase materials and enable children and adults to "read" what's inside.

Beginning the Journey with Children

At a morning meeting with the whole class, we ask, "Have you noticed some of the materials that have been coming into the classroom lately? We've found objects and materials that look interesting and fun to use, and we thought that maybe you and your parents would like to join us on this treasure hunt to find materials for our studio area."

We also decide that we need to send something tangible and practical home with the children for collecting. We prepare a bag for each child with Rita Harris' poem (see p. 2) stapled to it. We include a list of materials to give parents a few ideas about materials.

Dear Parents,

Kids from Group A want to collect! Would you help us?

When you are looking in drawers, you might find some things that we could use for projects. When you are putting out your "recycle stuff" or are outside walking, you might find some small things. We want to collect! We are going to bring bags home to collect our stuff. Please help us find things like broken jewelry, ribbons, feathers, metal and plastic things, clear or white containers—many things could do! The list that we are bringing home has more ideas.

Love,
Kids from Group A

Materials to Collect

wire
feathers
beads and buttons
costume jewelry
broken jewelry
tape
string
ribbon and yarn
old keys
small machines that don't work (i.e, watches and clocks)
corks and bottle caps
leather remnants
plastic sock holders
razor blade holders and other extruded objects

shells
sponges
small seed pods
wood scraps
containers: preferably white or transparent
baskets
cardboard pieces: all kinds and shapes, but not with writing or print
paper of different weights, textures, and colors
nails
screws and bolts
small mirrors

Safety Note

Please use great care and good judgment when collecting and using materials with young children. Parents should carefully determine that materials are clean and not sharp, toxic, or potentially harmful before allowing young children to use them. Be sure to keep small items away from very young children. Children under the age of three or four often put small objects in their mouths, creating a potential choking harzard.

"Where do you think this golden circle came from?"

The teacher offers an invitation to students: "If you would like to help write a letter to parents, you can stay on the rug after the meeting is over."

Creating Anticipation

Bags begin to collect in a special area in the classroom. We place a sign to make the area noticeable.

In response to the poem on the bags and the excitement of the children and parents, the table fills up. Both children and parents are eager to show their treasures. We didn't realize that parents would become so involved, but they seem as interested as the children. They want to see what other families have discovered.

Clipping the bags shut is a good way to keep the contents together. To maintain a sense of expectation, we wait until most of the bags are back before opening them.

"Wait till you see what's in my bag! You can look in the little hole and see what's in it. Maybe you can have a little peek. Look, it came from my own sparkle wand—look, twist paper."

Annie and her Mom arrive early one morning. Annie's Mom says, "I think that this is one of the most fun projects we have done. It made Annie look at things differently—as potential materials. It was exciting. She had some seam binding with tiny violets embroidered on it that was very special to her. Since she had two pieces, she decided to put one of them in her bag to share, and keep the other one at home in her collage box."

A Grand Opening

The day before our grand opening, we have a meeting with the teachers to plan the opening of the bags. We gather our containers and our own bags of found materials. We decide who is going to lead the discussion, who is going to observe and take notes, and who will take photos. We buy more film and blank tapes for the tape recorder. We even find a video camera. We don't want to let significant moments of discovery vanish without a record. Images and recordings help us gather memories to refer to in the future.

We really don't know what to expect, but we are prepared to be flexible. We are all interested and excited to find out what will happen.

Teacher: "Group A, I took one of these bags home, just like you did, and I looked, and I searched, and I hoped to see something that appealed to me…I found some interesting shapes and colors, and I put them in my bag and brought them to school. In just a few minutes we are going to get our bags and empty them in a big pile."

Matty: "They'll get all mixed up."

Hannah: "I know. We'll put out our mats and we'll put them far away from

Teachers invite children to empty their bags one at a time.

each other and we'll get our bags and empty them in front of us and look at what appeals to each of us!"

Teacher: "What do you think of mixing them all up in one big pile so we can all see what appeals to each and all of us?"

Children: "Yeah! Yeah!"

Teacher: "Before we begin, does anyone have a story about special or interesting things that happened while collecting?"

Emma: "I found some of my old toys that I broke a while ago and I put them in my bag."

Annie: "I found some candy wrappers and ribbon and some papers."

Collecting, Discovering, and Organizing Materials

Hannah: "The clock wasn't working at my house. We took the batteries out and I put it in my bag."

Matty: "We could open up the clock and see the little parts of the machine and how it works."

Caitlin: "We couldn't take any of my sister's stuff."

Jeremy: "I found some Styrofoam that you can press down and make stars with. I found some pressing things that were sitting outside."

Teacher: "We are getting lots of good ideas and we haven't even seen what's in our bags. Now, if you didn't bring a bag, that's ok. We can all share."

Children eagerly watch the pile grow.

Making Observations

The teacher decides to help the children focus their observations.

Teacher: "It is so exciting! Let's try something else. Look at all of the things in the middle of the rug. Think about what looks especially interesting or curious to you. Then, tell me something that you notice…something that appeals to you."

Gabriela: "The pine cone."

A teacher records the conversations and interactions in the classroom.

Mulu: "Keys."

Roger: "The golf ball."

Teacher: "We have this pile of beautiful stuff. Everyday things and things I've never seen before. What are we going to do with it all?"

Children: "Play in it."

Teacher: "If we play in our materials, they would get crushed. But your idea of playing is a good one. Let's play a sorting game. What do you think about sorting this pile of exciting, wonderful, colorful materials into smaller piles?"

Children: "Yes!"

Teacher: "Roger, I see that you are ready with an idea. How could we start sorting?"

Roger: "We'd take the things, and then put them somewhere, and then the pile would get smaller and smaller and smaller. And the pile would get so small, so small, that nothing's in the middle!"

Teacher: "So what would you want to choose first?"

Roger: "Golf balls."

Teacher: "Ok, Roger, why don't you begin our sorting by collecting anything that's a ball—anything that is round. Children, you should be thinking of what things you would like to sort because I will ask you in a minute. Roger, if I got you a little tray, would that make it easier for you?"

Jeremy: "Roger, here are some balls. Over here."

Annie: "Hey, here's some wallpaper!"

Teacher: "Would anyone like to make a pile of wallpaper? Annie, here is a tray for you to collect wallpaper."

Miriam: "I want to make a pile of ribbons."

Caitlin: "I want to collect paper."

Teacher: "How about you, Emma? What would you like to collect?"

Emma: "I want to collect jewelry."

Teacher: "What would you like to collect, Mulu?"

Mulu: "Metal."

Teacher: "Great idea. Does anyone see any metal for Mulu?"

Annie: "I found keys. Here, Mulu."

Arthur: "I'm collecting wood."

Jeremy: "Oh, fabric!"

Teacher: "Sit back and give these children a chance to collect! It will be your turn very soon."

Robert: "I'm tired of looking."

After hearing this comment, the teacher suggests: "If you feel like you have done enough sorting, come with me. We will talk about making other choices. If you want to come back later, when there are not so many children sorting, you can do that, too." While watching the children, we realize that, for some of them, the experience is a little overwhelming. We agree that next time we will invite children to open their bags in small groups.

Recording a list of the categories that children have identified is a way to remember together.

Noticing, Sorting, Categorizing

After watching children pick out and study one item after another—commenting on it, guessing what it is and where it came from—it is clear that the children's main interest is in looking, feeling, comparing, describing, contrasting, and exchanging observations with one another. They are really not interested in making anything yet.

By standing back, observing, and recording the children's discussions, teachers learn that children have unique and unexpected ways of organizing, categorizing, and describing—ways adults may not have even considered. Being open and attentive to the fresh and unusual ways in which children think is to be open to new ideas. This is one of the ways in which adults can learn from children. But these moments often pass, unnoticed or forgotten, if not recorded.

As they make decisions about each object and which category it fits, children are learning about the characteristics of different materials and using a rich descriptive vocabulary.

We find that it is important to have a clipboard, pad and pen, or a tape recorder in an accessible place.

Jeremy concentrates on collecting all of the yarn.

"It's like a puzzle! It fits together."

Mulu experiments with pieces of the pink Styrofoam stuff that his friend, Jeremy, brought in his bag.

Listening to Children's Thoughts

Even at this beginning stage of exploring, we find out some of the children's interests. Ideas for future explorations or projects begin to appear. In talking over the experience, reading through notes, and listening to a section of the tape recording, we pull out what we think are significant moments to revisit. In the process, we become more aware of what children are thinking and wondering about. Our respect for these young people grows, and we add new ideas to our image of the children who we teach, but who also teach us. We realize that it is this interaction between experience and analysis that keeps the learning process going.

Discovering properties of plastic:

Jaimie: "That goes in there. I think we have plastic...where is that plastic? I think it is down here. This is plastic too."

Arthur: "No it's not!"

Jaimie: "It has plastic in it."

Arthur: "Ok."

Jaimie: "A flashlight! It's broken. It's plastic."

Thoughts about an antique nail:

Thomas observes a large nail brought in by a parent who collects antiques: "Where did this come from? I think this is a nail that got shaved—a huge nail. You probably could use it to put boats together...It's so old and dusty, so it might be from a train track. No one knows."

Testing hypotheses:
Stephen: "I found something that's metal. These are metal because I can feel they're metal."
Taylor: "Can I feel them? You're right, Stephen, they are metal!"
Annie makes a metaphor: "The silver wire is like the silver friend. The gold wire is like the gold friend."(The class sang, "Make new friends, but keep the old; One is silver and the other's gold" earlier in the morning.)
Caitlin: "Cardboard, cardboard! Do you think we need another category? You know what we should do? We can use all the stuff to decorate the whole school."
Matty: "Do you know what my favorite thing is? The watch."
Hannah, as she picks up a make-up brush: "Maybe we could have a salon!"
Masaye: "Let's make music! Listen, these beads make music."

"Let's make music! Listen, these beads make music."

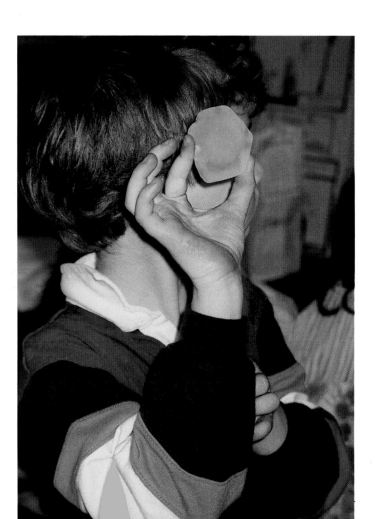

As a group, the children list categories for the materials.

Revisiting the Experience

At the end of the morning, children and teachers gather to see what has happened to the materials. The teacher reads through the list of categories while children look over the containers of sorted materials.

We observe that the children seem to build attachments to the materials without having to own them.

Here is the children's list of categories:

balls	outside stuff
paper	plastic stuff
fabric	dinosaurs
hearts	wrapping paper
seashells	yarn
stars	straws
metal	soft and curly things
wood	music-making things
ribbon	salon things
flowers	corks
buttons	sparkling stuff
keys	
jewelry	
tops	

Some categories have only a few items. Ribbons and plastic materials are the most numerous.

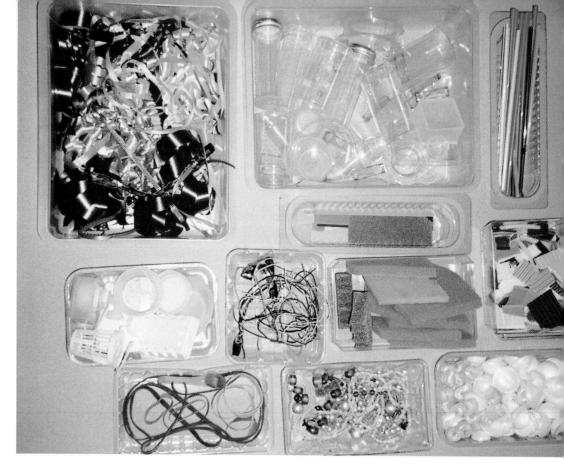

Our Beautiful Materials

At the end of the day, teachers and a few children move and consolidate the materials. Together, we notice how beautiful and enticing the materials have become. We arrange and rearrange the materials many times. Each time that we do this, we discover new possibilities and take pleasure in the details that come to our attention. We notice how the clear and white containers enhance the beauty and distinctive qualities of each material. We realize that the more materials we collect, the more the categories will change and become more defined.

Involving parents

As parents pick up their children, they admire our collections. At this point, more in-depth looking and discovery begins. Children, teachers, and parents are all getting new ideas about potential materials. In the following days, weeks, and throughout the year, parents and children enjoy contributing to the room by bringing in carefully chosen materials and containers.

As materials get out of order, we invite children to playfully place them back in order.

Collecting, Discovering, and Organizing Materials

Sorting materials into categories as children bring them into the room is an excellent way to make the transition between home and school. It is a way to let go of materials. It also immediately engages the child and parent in a task.

Arthur adds materials from his bag to our collections as he comes in the room. He considers where he will place each of his treasures.

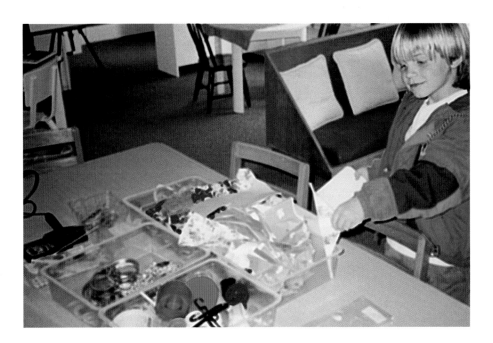

Creating Order

Whenever materials come into the room, there is work to do. Cutting out the usable parts of wrapping paper and other materials helps to make materials small enough to see, store, and use.

Annie spots some wrapping paper she wants to use to make a dress for her Lady. "I want to use some of that gorgeous paper to make a gorgeous lady. I'm going to use some sparkling things, too." To realize her idea, she needs to find a way to make her paper smaller. In order to solve this problem, Annie uses and, in the process, practices her cutting skills.

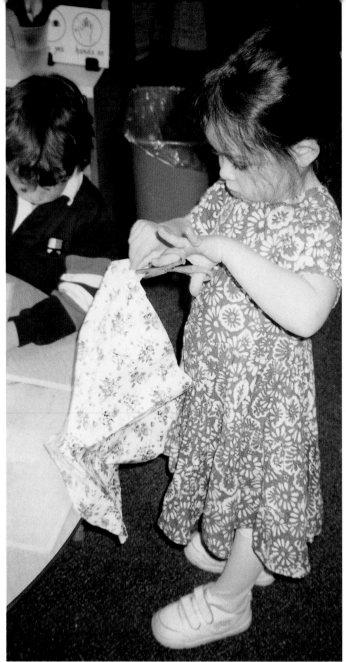

Cutting is a very important skill to work on in the early years. The desire to use some of this beautiful paper is a strong motivator for Annie.

Cutting out the unwrinkled and untaped parts of wrapping paper is a great way to collect interesting papers.

There are always materials that are just too cumbersome to keep or that you simply do not want. Since clutter is so distracting, teachers inevitably have to make selections and throw some materials away. Being discreet about this saves hurt feelings on the part of both children and parents.

On some days, a pan of soapy water and a pan of clean water is available for children to wash and dry an assortment of materials. Children need and want "real" jobs, and they enjoy doing them. They know that cleaning materials is important work, because the materials aren't usable or appealing if they are not clean. They work out ways to cooperate to get the job done, and, in the process, they get to know the materials better.

Setting Up a Studio Space

The typical art corner in many classrooms has supplies such as crayons, markers, scissors, staplers, tape, paste, and glue sticks. All of these supplies can be enhanced by careful selection, making them available in interesting and attractive ways, and including found objects and natural materials with them. A variety of quality papers and different drawing materials open up other options. Storing materials in clear or white containers allows children to clearly see the colors and textures of each material. In the same way, when furniture, walls, and shelves are white or neutral, the nature of the materials stored there is more evident.

In the words of Loris Malaguzzi, the founder of the schools for young children in Italy's Reggio Emilia, "The atelier, in our approach, is an additional space within the school where to explore with our hands and our minds, and where to refine our sight..." (*The Hundred Languages of Children*, p. 143.)

A laboratory for thinking

The studio space is not an isolated place where artistic things happen. It is a "laboratory for thinking." It is a place to see that thinking can be expressed through materials. In order for this to happen, it is important to create a space where materials are visible and easy to reach so that there is the possibility for children to return to what they were doing and follow up on ideas. To have a special space where children can concentrate on their work with materials is conducive to learning and to children finding their own strengths.

The ideal space allows time for ideas to percolate overnight or longer so that new enthusiasm and new solutions to perplexing problems might grow and be tried out. Just leaving one shelf blank for children's work, unfinished or finished, creates a relationship between the children and the area. That shelf becomes a little display area for children to visit. It also serves to inspire discussions between children. It is a way for children to get to know one another through their work. We encourage children to arrange their work attractively as they place it on the shelf.

It is important for children to participate in setting up and maintaining the studio space, but at carefully chosen times and with the support of teachers. Sorting and organizing, editing, cleaning, displaying, and keeping order are lifelong skills. As the seasons and needs change, and as materials are used up and new materials contributed to the classroom, the studio area needs to be reorganized and rearranged. Helping teachers and parents with these tasks gives children the opportunity to use and develop all of these skills, and to experience the pleasure of being in an aesthetic environment.

A corner of the classroom can become a space for exploration, a quiet space for thinking, and a protected space. When materials are organized and attractively presented, the space becomes an invitation to children. They enjoy not only working with the materials, but also handling them and keeping them in order. Storing materials in containers makes them easily accessible as well as easy to put away.

What We Learned...

About introducing the materials:

We all thought a great deal about how to choreograph this initial experience. We realized that we were actually constructing a situation that would affect the social life in the classroom. Care was needed in how we introduced materials. We were very worried about the amount of materials that the children would bring in and how we were going to handle large quantities. Now, we agree that the bags were a good idea, and a good size, because they limited amounts.

About collecting:

The children seemed to have a natural desire to collect and study materials, but we, as teachers, needed to understand the properties of materials before we could begin collecting. The time we spent gathering and playing with the materials ourselves helped us to feel comfortable enough to begin this journey with children.

About sorting:

Even though we knew that these materials were very interesting, we just didn't realize how intrigued the children would be and how much time they would want to spend just looking and touching. Sorting was a good vehicle for channeling and nurturing this desire to observe in an organized way. Sorting kept children interested in the materials. We noticed that the children treated all found objects well and handled them delicately. By giving the materials this kind of attention they became precious things. We observed that the sorting process also gave children a vehicle for connecting with one another.

About communication:

We soon realized that an enthusiastic adult has to be involved to keep the communication and dialogue going. The kinds of questions to ask as well as when to ask or make an observation became very important parts of being present to the moment with children. As we looked back at the children's conversations, we were struck by how many of the children's interests we hadn't been aware of before. Even at this early stage, we noticed several interesting questions and themes emerging.

At this point:

Our overwhelming feeling is that the whole experience was so rich, so exciting, and a great way to engage parents.

Chapter 2

Exploring Materials

*E*ach material has unique characteristics. Exploring gives children and adults a vehicle for discovering those properties. Exploring also means figuring out what a particular material can do. Can it bend? How much? Can it hold its shape? Stack? Stand up by itself?

Young children have a natural sense of design that is especially evident in the early years. It is this design sense that a great number of twentieth-century artists have tried to recapture in their own work. If given the opportunity and time to explore, children naturally order objects by size, categorize objects by color or shape, and differentiate between objects that are straight and curved, rough and smooth, flat or rounded. As children manipulate objects, they often arrange them symmetrically, in radiating configurations, and in compositions that depict real things such as landscapes, machines, people, and animals.

When we, as teachers, take time to explore these materials together, we begin to truly see their potential.

Exploring materials is an evocative experience. It stimulates the imagination. It invites children to tell stories and to develop games. Social interaction is a natural outcome of exploring. Exploring materials is also a bridge to other avenues of expression, such as drawing, collage, construction, and sculpture.

*"Let's build another tower—
a tower of caps!"
"Let's make a pattern: black
cap, top; black cap, top."*

Children delight in discovering
materials and finding new friendships.

First Encounters

After spending a morning observing the children opening bags, and then several days continuing the sorting process in small groups, we realize that children obviously enjoy touching, examining, and comparing materials, but just aren't ready to move to the more intense sorting that we have planned. Instead, the children seem to have their own pace and way of working. We learn where to go next by observing what they are doing.

Becoming sensitive to children's pace and interests

The children carefully pick up and examine one object at a time. They turn it around, study it, and often talk about it. Then they lay the object down carefully next to them. It is almost as if they are introducing each new object into their own personal inventory of experience. As they explore each new object, it becomes part of a carefully arranged little display on the floor beside them. We decide to build upon this observation during the following days.

To provide a framework, we give each child a piece of construction paper on which to work. We put out containers of the smaller materials all mixed together on the table or floor. Because we are working with a class of eighteen children all at the same time, and want to be sure that there are enough materials to look through, we ask children to begin by choosing up to eight objects that they find especially interesting. Once they have several objects that they like—and they can always switch objects or add more materials from the other boxes—they can make a display of the objects to show to their friends. We plan to visit all of the displays.

Finding a small plastic chess piece prompts Taylor to think, and then to say, "Hey cool. I made a little game. It really is a game. You move this to a spot and then you ask a question. Then you move this to another spot and then you ask another question. Hey guys, you know what? I'll show you how to play the game. You move it to a spot, and then you ask it a question." Taylor experiments further with his arrangement before he returns the objects to the container.

Teaching is learning

It is a learning experience for us to watch this exploration take place. The children are totally absorbed by all the treasures. The tone in the room changes to a quiet hum. The little set-ups that children create are varied and inventive. Some children choose only a few items and stop. Some keep going and going until their entire papers are full. Some children are so involved in looking at the materials that they never get around to arranging at all—and this is all right! We discovered so many exciting and interesting things about children's interests, intelligence, and ways of working—and about our own insecurities by standing back and observing.

From our own experiences while exploring, we anticipate the children's delight, but not their deep interest. See what happens to Annie's set-up on the next page.

We observe that younger children, or those encountering the materials for the first time, seem to separate objects. They seem to want to give each object its own space.

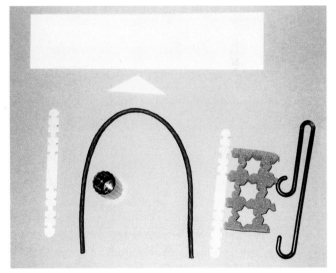

We try to document, through photographs and written observations, examples of arrangements that we expect as well as examples that we do not expect.

Design Sense

Looking at these arrangements of objects, we see the strong sense of design in young children. It is this sense of composition that Picasso refers to when he says, "Once I drew like Raphael, but it has taken me a whole lifetime to learn how to draw like children." The strong sense of design that emerges in the early years is often misunderstood or not encouraged. To hear children describe how they put together their designs helps us appreciate the complexity of their thinking and their many ways of making connections.

Emma looks at this photo and says, "I remember that Hannah and I wanted the same thing, so we found one for each of us. Instead of saying, 'Oh, I was using that,' I would say, 'you can use it, I'll find another.' Hannah was giving something to me right there."

"I made an insect!"

The class has been engaged in a study of insects. One child designed this insect while arranging his materials. He made a connection between the classroom study of insects and the materials he was exploring. The shape characteristics of the found materials reminded him of the three body parts of the insect.

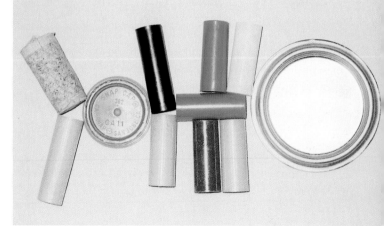

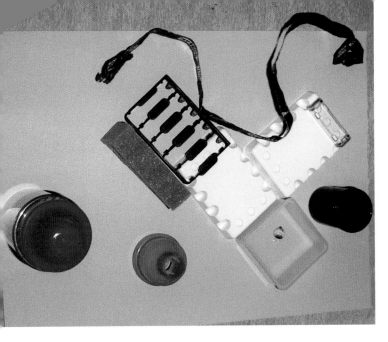

Jeremy recognized this photograph right away. He said, "I was trying to find ones that you match together."

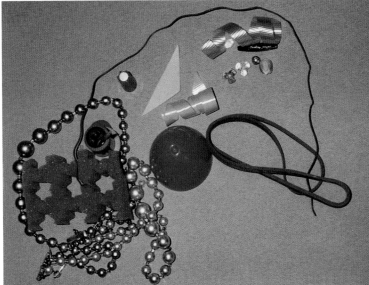

"It's an elephant....He's rearing up."

This is Annie's completed set-up that she began with Gracie. When she saw this photograph she said, "It's an elephant. You can see his two teeny, tiny eyes (orange beads) and his two teeny, tiny legs (silver beads). See his trunk (rubber band)? He's rearing up."

After children become more familiar with materials, they tend to combine them, to make objects touch, and to construct with them.

Universal Designs

Because adults recognize and feel comfortable with symmetrical and radial designs, they tend to see them more often than other, more subtle types of arrangements. Rhoda Kellogg, in a thorough study of children's visual representations, found that a number of configurations are universal in young children's work. Among these configurations are shapes, symmetrical and radial designs, mandalas, and suns. We encourage children to "save a memory" of their configurations by drawing them.

Isabelle chooses to work with craft sticks and toothpicks from the box of wooden things. She develops her own sense of order: toothpicks in the corners, sticks on the sides.

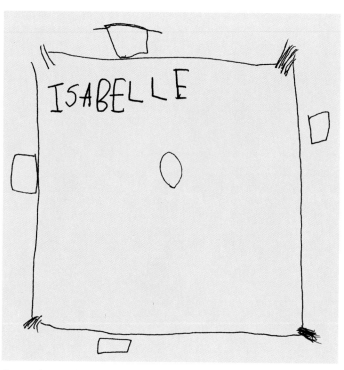

Several months later, Isabelle looks at a photograph of her arrangement and decides to draw it. "I just like to make designs," she says.

Does the shape of the surface influence the way that children arrange objects? We asked ourselves these kinds of questions as we made different shapes of paper available.

Abby reconstructs her symmetrical design as she draws it. Going from one language to another—from construction to drawing, for example—can help children make their ideas clearer.

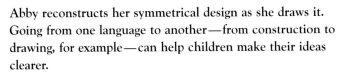

Telling Stories with Metal Things

Materials are suggestive. As children place similar things in one container and continue to add to them, subtle differences in shape, color, and texture begin to show themselves.

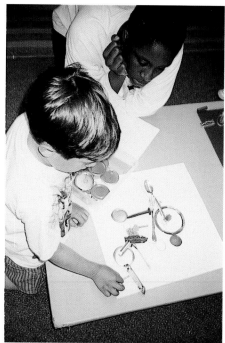

As children continue to place "metal things" in a container, the objects gleam and glisten.

Robert's teacher notices that he is deeply engaged in arranging his metallic set-up. She also notices that he has connected all of his pieces. She listens, observes, and records Robert's story: "It's like a maze." Robert picks up a little square piece of chain-linked metal and says, "That's the knight. That's where it started. You have to go through the kitchen. That's the refrigerator. That's a road. There's another road. Those copper things are all bridges."

"Suns"

The sun configuration, which is not necessarily representative of the solar sun, is often the first recognizable configuration that young children draw.

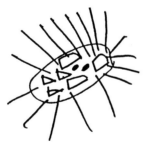

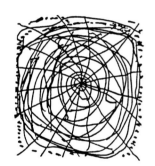

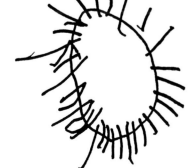

Thomas, who has been working with many materials, decides to explore the metal things. "I'm going to make a person. Cool. It's like a ring...so pretty...I'm really making a sun. It's a design in the middle. It's still a sun. This is my little workshop over here."

"Suns," or lines crossing the perimeter of a shape, are often used by children to draw trees, plants, and hands—as in this drawing of a little person.

Thinking about Circles

Drawing circles grows out of scribbling experiences. The circle is usually the first shape that young children between the ages of three and four draw. As teachers observe this miracle taking place, they save children's work.

This child is captivated by her discovery. She draws variations of circles—big, medium, and little ones—circles inside of circles and circles around circles. For many days, she continues to practice her newly found skill. She fills many sheets of paper with circles.

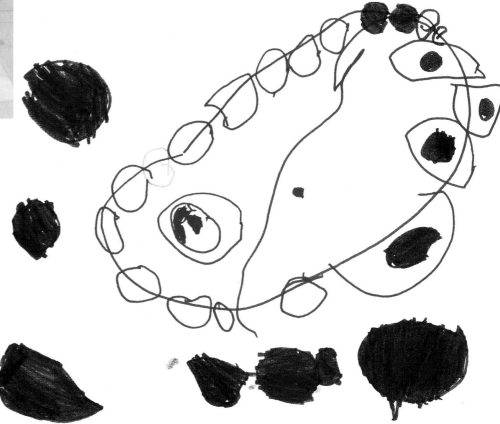

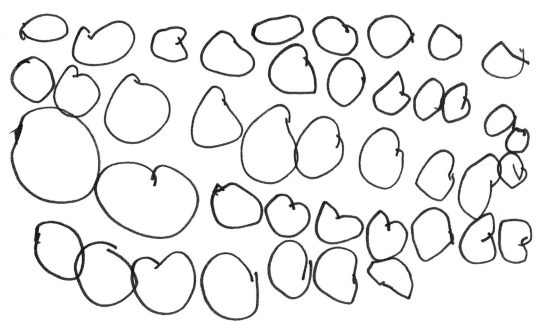

As often happens with a new discovery by one child, interest in circles seems to be catching. Children in the room draw and pick out circles from the recycled materials in the studio area. We provide containers for them to fill with round objects.

More Investigations of Circles

When the children come back the next morning, they find their boxes of circle objects along with containers of objects that the teacher has added.

"I think it looks like a million eyes!"

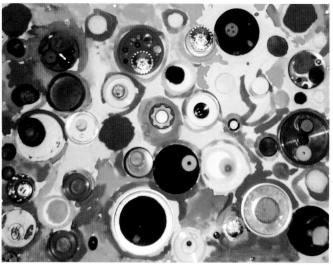

The teacher sets up a situation as a way of stimulating children to continue their investigation of circular forms.

A group of children arranged and glued circular objects onto a large piece of cardboard. The next day, they painted the spaces so that the objects would stand out.

One child discovers that her dress is filled with circles and goes to the easel to experiment with her idea in another medium. We decide to try this kind of exploration with other shapes.

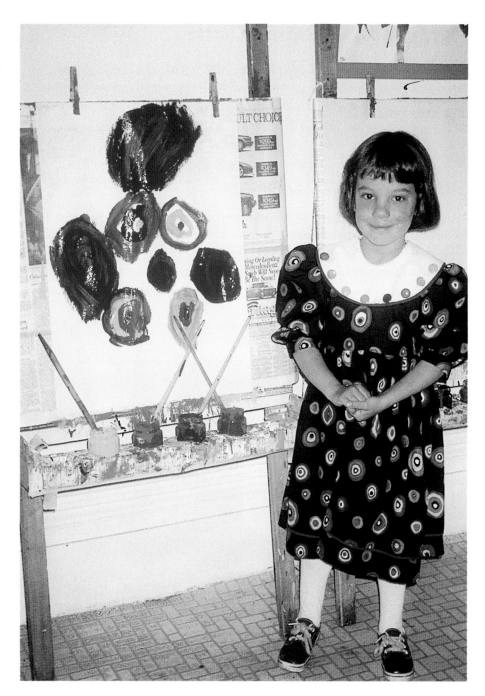

Sorting by Color

Sorting is an experience that grows more refined as the days and weeks progress. This exploration begins as a group of three- and four-year-old girls pull "pink stuff" from all the containers in the room. The teacher asks them if they would like to sort other colors as well, and makes more containers available.

Building on the comments of children

A tape recorder captures the words of the children and their interactions. It becomes the ears of the teacher in areas where children are working on their own or when a teacher is listening and observing, but events are happening quickly. By transcribing the recorded tape, we rediscover children's thoughts. We find them useful when continuing the exploration later in the day. These transcribed thoughts also help parents get involved.

Hannah: "Pink is part of the red family. It goes in the red box. Dark pink…a water thing."

Ariana: "I'm not going to put that color in here because it's kind of orangeish."

Jack: "Orange and green are my favorite colors. Actually, I like the whole rainbow."

Steven: "Hey, another gray. I'm getting all the grays out. Look, a key! Where's the metal stuff?"

A teacher in training learns to appreciate the complexity of children's ideas as she records their stories, thoughts, and interactions.

The teacher observes this group of girls who are repeatedly drawn to the color pink. She finds a way to challenge them to take that interest further by making their study of pink into a more complex and discriminating activity.

Jamie talks as she arranges objects from the yellow container, "You have to hop or walk from next to next. But, everywhere you go, there's something...It's a big sun with yellow dots all around it...These are yellow bees."

Broadening the Exploration of Color

The teacher has saved Chloe and Jamie's set-ups from the morning. Here, Chloe explains what she was doing to the rest of the class. Then Chloe and her teacher suggest a sorting procedure. After sorting, the children choose one color box and arrange the objects on one of the large papers set out in the classroom.

When the group of girls join their classmates and friends on the playground, they tell about sorting colors. A few other children seem interested in trying that experience. Once they are back in the classroom, the teachers and children together set up a sorting and arranging activity and invite the class to try it.

Saving traces

Photographs of the exploration and the arrangements become valuable tools for remembering the experience and extending it. Later these photos, along with the comments of the children, are displayed in the classroom. The teacher's explanation of how this exploration unfolded, and the rationale behind it, communicates to parents and other colleagues the importance of learning with materials.

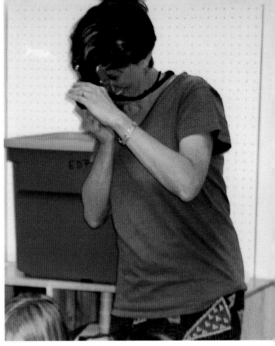

A teacher photographs the experience to share with parents and other teachers.

Children enjoy spreading out objects on large sheets of construction paper. Because there are now so many objects in each color box, the larger papers give them more room. Smaller papers, on the other hand, might encourage children to build and work three-dimensionally.

Carlos arranges objects from the red box on a large piece of black paper. He then changes boxes with Steven and works on an arrangement of black objects.

The Work-in-Process Shelf

Studio materials are moved around as investigations change and grow. Now, instead of working with the whole class, the teachers move the boxes of color objects into the studio area so that children can continue to build upon their initial interest and design ideas. A work-in-process shelf welcomes, invites, and allows children to continue their work. It communicates respect for children's work and for the process of thinking and taking time.

A shelf for work in process encourages children to take time to return to their explorations and bring them to a more complex level. "In process" suggests that work can continue. Here you see Carlos setting up the blue objects which he didn't have a chance to try the previous day because other children were using them.

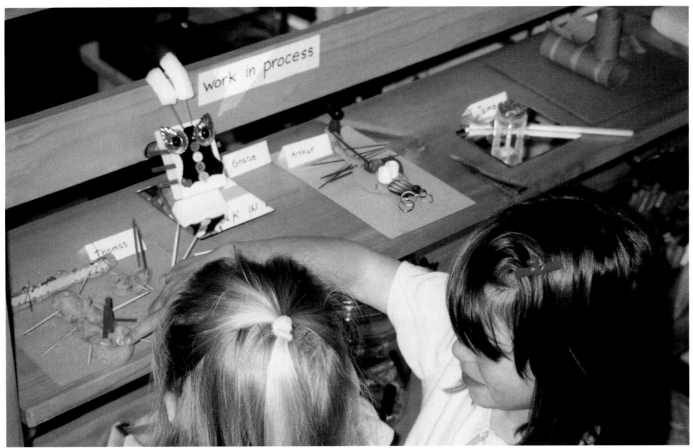

Children look at and discuss insects made from clay and found materials. Work on display by classmates provokes conversations and new ideas.

Children have different rhythms. Some work until a task is completed. Some concentrate very hard, but need to take time out before being able to continue such deep concentration. Having the possibility to return to what they were doing respects children's different ways of working.

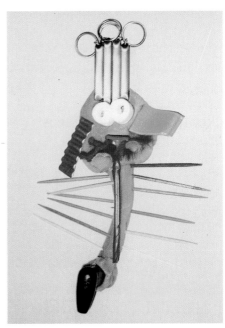

Here's a close-up of one of the clay insects on the shelf.

What We Learned...

Using the boxes of objects sorted by color, pairs of children arranged the materials into a giant rainbow of colors, glued them to white paper, and returned a week later to paint all the white spaces.

About exploring:

The exploratory part of this experience was the biggest unknown for us, and also the most fascinating. We had been looking for ways to encourage and extend experimentation and exploration because we knew that these kinds of experiences are so satisfying to children. Often, we think children need to make something to have when, in fact, we saw the opposite. Some children were interested in constructing with the materials, while some children just enjoyed studying one object at a time. Some children seemed to be interested in design and in setting up a pleasing composition. Other children used the materials to tell a story.

About skill levels:

We observed that when children did something that required fine motor skills, the differences between children's skill levels were strong. But when children experimented with found materials, the differences in skill levels were narrowed. Of course, a nurturing teacher who delighted in the children's inventions and encouraged the exchange of ideas—even when she didn't know what to expect—helped narrow the gap.

About renewing interest:

The idea of experimenting with materials as a group, and then moving them to a new place, perhaps the studio area, was one way to keep the experience alive. Arranging the materials invitingly in their new space helped draw children back to the experience.

About saving the experience:

Saving a trace or a memory of an experience is so important to the art of learning and teaching. Displaying children's arrangements was one logical and very effective way to do this. Teachers asked children to discuss their arrangements. Teachers also used sketches and photographs to save images. Photos of children at work helped parents see and understand the children's deep interest in working with the materials. Direct quotes from children or transcriptions of a tape recording that explain the photos and set-ups became an effective reference point for parents. Children loved to hear their teachers read back a dialogue. These dialogues sparked renewed interest.

At this point:

In this chapter, you can see the importance and value of recording children's experiences and insights as part of the learning process for children and teachers alike. The process of documentation parallels the children's process of discovery.

Chapter 3

Connections

Encounters with materials give children many ideas and spark connections. The ideas continue to develop as children move through the day, leave school, visit other places, and enter their homes. Collecting materials and ideas for a project on one day, then inviting children to wait overnight to think them through, builds a sense of anticipation and allows for changes in plans and new ideas. The same process is also true for teachers. When children and teachers return to school, the possibility should exist for them to work with these new ideas and share their thinking and excitement with one another.

"I'm going to make a puppet with very big eyes. His eyes go out so far! These are ears. That's the mouth on top. Now I have my puppet."

Roger proudly displays the puppet that he has created.

Taking a Risk

Teachers know the powerful learning potential of puppets. We propose that children make puppets from the materials in our studio. Instead of giving children a model on which to base their puppets, however, we decide to take a chance. We will not show a "way" to do it. Instead, we ask, "How could you make a puppet from our materials?" We encourage the children to take a moment to think about the materials that we have been exploring.

The children share many ideas. We refrain from giving directions. (This is difficult for us.) Instead, we distribute materials as in our earlier explorations. We ask the children to pick out eight objects that they think they will use to build their puppets, and begin to arrange them. We put boxes of smaller materials on the tables and boxes of larger materials, such as cardboard, toilet paper rolls, and mat board scraps, in the back of the room.

These are beginning ideas and we want the children to have time to think about this idea of puppets. We encourage them to walk around the room to visit each other's arrangements. Instead of distributing glue, we give each child a little box with his or her name where they can store their materials and return to work on them the following day. This also gives us time to figure out what we will do next.

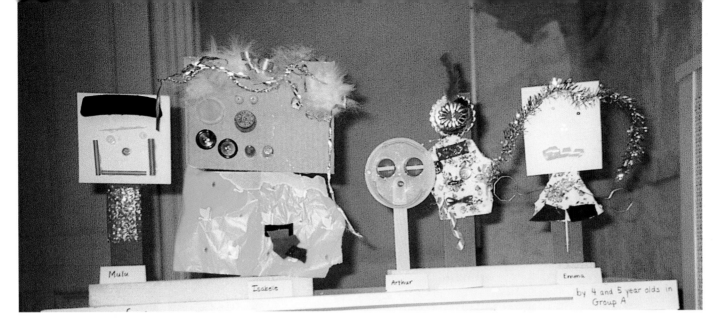

Supporting children's ideas and constructions

Children become very familiar with objects as they notice, collect, sort, and arrange them. When they encounter a problem, such as how to make a puppet, they remember the characteristics of the materials that they observed and touched, and they make connections. To support our new way of working, we observe and take careful notes of what children say. Teachers decide to use a glue gun to support the work of two children at a time. As children rearrange their puppets and ideas, one of us attaches objects.

Finished puppets displayed in a Styrofoam stand highlight each child's construction while giving children easy accessibility for dramatization of stories.

Jaimie remembers the faucet she brought in from home. When working side by side, children delight in the inventions of their classmates and get to know one another in unexpected ways.

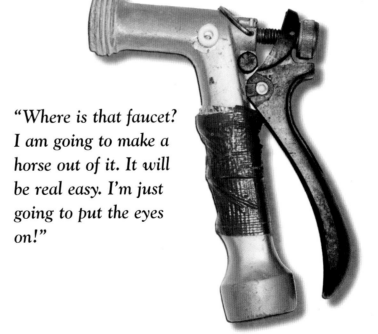

"Where is that faucet? I am going to make a horse out of it. It will be real easy. I'm just going to put the eyes on!"

51

This box of "sparkly" things kindles a child's imagination.

A Child and a Marionette

Gracie takes great pleasure in looking through the box of sparkling treasures. She gathers more and more ribbons and glitter and threads from this box of materials that simply fascinates her. What is she going to do? What is she thinking? Does she have a plan or is she simply touching and exploring?

Gracie begins to tie her treasures together in different ways. The teachers notice her tying and attaching skills.

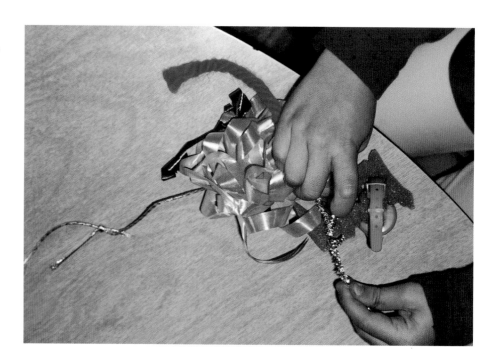

Gracie isn't finished yet. She continues to think about how to animate her assemblage.

When Gracie ties the orange piece of yarn onto her cluster of ribbons, she says: "Those are the legs!" She has figured out her own unique way to make a dancing princess.

A Study of Faces

After many drawing and scribbling experiences, preprimary children become interested in representation. They begin to turn their circular shapes into faces and into their first images of people.

To take advantage of this natural progression, the teacher sets up a situation with materials that she feels can lead to a more extended exploration of faces. She places many interesting objects, and many pairs of objects, into containers. When the children gather around, she asks them to take the objects from the boxes and set them out so that they can see them.

Mirrors invite children to draw their own faces.

Teacher and child explore the face and its features together.

"Two black eyes. I see cheeks. I see ears."

As Isabelle and Miriam lay out their materials, the teacher records their conversation.

Isabelle: "Hey, look at this…this is from outside…This piece looks like a ladder."

Miriam: "There's two of each. These match, so they go over here. This one doesn't match, so it goes in the middle."

Isabelle: "Two black eyes. I see cheeks. I see ears."

Miriam: "I see ponytails…a mouth…eyebrows. Here's a forehead."

From her many observations of children, the teacher knows that when they come across matching pairs of objects, children often see them as eyes. She sets up a situation that she thinks will lead children to return to their earlier thoughts about possible facial features. Recycled objects tend to make unique features.

The materials act as springboards for exploration.

Transforming Objects into Facial Features

In preparing for this experience, the teachers ask themselves many questions, "Do children need the suggestion of a face shape to work on, or is it better to give them a rectangle? If we do give the children an oval, how big should it be? What color would be appropriate?" We decide to give children a choice of large oval papers in a variety of colors, but there are many other possibilities that we look forward to trying out another time.

The teacher extends the exploration by asking Miriam and Isabelle to use the mirror and their own faces as references before choosing and arranging objects.

Miriam builds a little face.

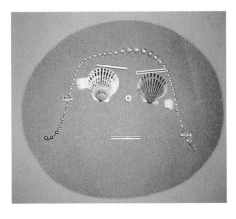

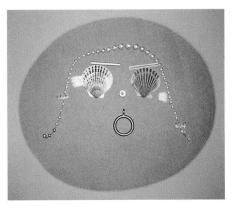

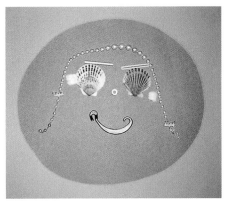

Miriam says, "This would make a perfect nose. This necklace could be hair!"

The teacher asks her to try changing one of the features to see what would happen.

She chuckles and tries choosing another object for the mouth.

Miriam decides that she needs something else to add and goes to the studio to look for other materials.

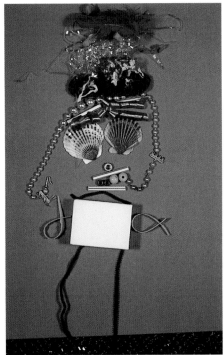

The teacher asks Miriam if she could make a new face without the oval shape underneath it. Miriam adds a body, arms, and legs and says, "She's going to a ball."

At the same time, Isabelle has been thinking about which objects she will use for her face. She notices some yellow plastic fasteners and says, "I need some lips, shivering lips." We observe that the shape of the object suggested this poetic adjective to Isabelle.

Collage Characters

Remembering the interest of both teachers and children in exploring and creating faces, the kindergarten teachers decide to use the exploratory process as a springboard for a more in-depth study. They experiment with the objects themselves in order to think through what materials they will offer to the children. They remember that children love to look through the containers of objects, and note that this takes time. It takes time and concentration to understand and work with the idea that one object can stand for, or be transformed into, another. They decide to keep a mirror handy so that children can research both features and expressions.

Collage boxes of small, light items with one flat side that can be easily attached by gluing are placed in the center of the table. The suggestive properties of materials allow for the expression of children's unique observations. Doug explains, "I did fur for lips because if you actually feel your lips, they're soft, like fur."

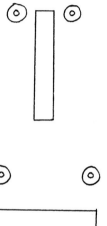

Creating two totally different arrangements is another way for children to discover that a slight movement of almost any feature can change the character and expression of the face.

In order to extend the exploration and make the task more intriguing, teachers ask children to experiment with changing the placement of a facial feature before they offer them glue.

By this time, the faces seem to have developed expressions and personalities. The character dries and awaits her body and clothes. Who will she become? Holding up each child's work and asking about something they might add gives children a chance to see what they have done from a new perspective, and to think about what they will do next. The time between one part of a project and the next allows ideas to emerge.

When they have finished experimenting, children glue the objects to a construction paper backing which provides a base and space for future work. It creates an expectation that more will be done.

New discoveries

Beginning by focusing only on the eyes and nose expands the possibility of thinking more deeply about the face and allows experimentation with placement. Another way to build children's investment in what they do is to engage them in conversation about their work.

After sorting out, handling, arranging, and gluing objects, children are more able to transform one language of expression into another by drawing.

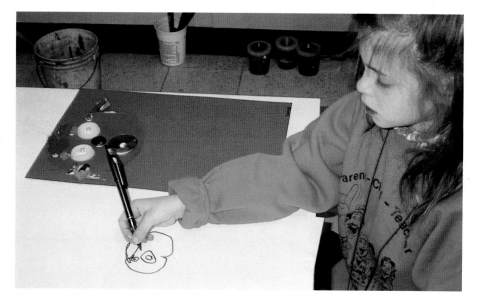

59

"What else will you add to your character? Is anything missing? What materials do you need?"

Adding Bodies and Clothing

Some children want to add a body to the faces that they made. We gather construction paper and our scrap box, and look in the studio for additional materials. The teacher waits to offer glue so that children can develop and refine their ideas. Children use many skills as they cut and arrange costumes and appendages. They make many decisions. Often, the first idea is modified by a new idea that presents itself as a child works.

All of the wrapping paper pieces are pulled out and examined as children gather materials to complete the bodies of their characters.

A child cuts and arranges the clothes of his collage person.

"I'm going to have a neck and a stomach. I'm wearing a plaid shirt with crazy arms."

"Does this match? I cut around the top to make shoulders. I'm having tights."

"I'm making Dorothy from *The Wizard of Oz.*"

"This looks funny to me. I'm going to put it here instead."

"I need some legs—I wonder what I can use for legs—maybe this. Now, where are those scissors?"

"These two things are the arms and these are the legs and this is the shirt. I like the shoes best because they're colorful."

"I cut the ears because I couldn't find the right shape. I just cut them out! I'm thinking about the buttons. One of the buttons is really tiny. I can't find the right pattern that goes with the shirt."

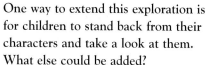

One way to extend this exploration is for children to stand back from their characters and take a look at them. What else could be added?

When all the parts are assembled, it is time to begin gluing. How to glue large pieces of paper is a problem for a young child. It's a real-life problem, too. It makes sense to introduce and discuss gluing skills when a real problem presents itself.

Drawing to Remember

The act of constructing seems to give children both visual and tactile understanding of form. Once children build a structure, they seem quite comfortable trying to draw it. The experience is a powerful one for children. It is a great way to help children realize and become aware of their potential and ability. Even those children who are reluctant to draw are usually very proud of their newly discovered skill.

After completing their collage characters, we ask the children to draw them.

One way to support children who have difficulty in drawing their collage characters is to suggest that they draw the parts of the characters in the order that they built them.

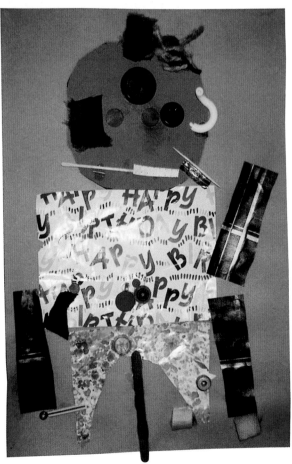

Connections

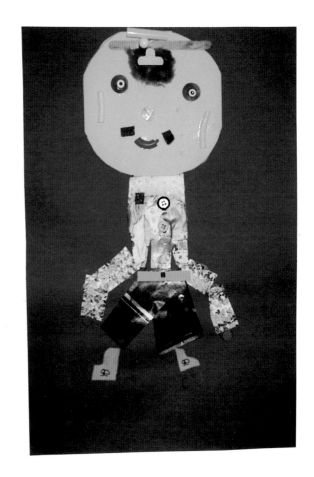

Max

These children begin paintings using their collage drawings as blueprints. They are moving into the free expressive language of paint and color as they once again revisit and add to their characters.

Extending the Exploration

In listening to the conversations among children, it is clear that complex personalities are being born. As the teachers listen to the children tell stories about their characters to one another, they ask the children if they would like to write down their stories.

This child added color to her brush-drawn character.

"My clown likes to juggle and his name is Silly Guy."

What We Learned…

About taking risks:

Leaving the "way" of making puppets open felt like a big risk. Deciding beforehand not to attach or glue anything right away helped all of us relax and enjoy the children's explorations and discoveries. It was interesting to see what materials different children chose and how they arranged them. Sometimes they didn't look like puppets to us at all, but we saw that the children were so pleased that we were led to study and appreciate their plans.

About problem solving:

Saving the children's selections in boxes gave us time to figure out how to proceed. We observed that many children didn't have a base for attaching objects, so we gathered cardboard scraps and other flat objects that we thought would be useful for bases. In most instances, the children figured out their own unique solutions.

About reflection:

By working on the puppets and the collages we learned to break the experiences down into smaller parts and to allow time for experimentation and reflection. Before returning to add to or construct the puppets or collages, we spent time together looking at the children's work in progress and listening to their ideas. We also read some of the descriptions that we had recorded in our notes. This time spent revisiting ongoing work from a new perspective and sharing observations and ideas with children also helped to build their interest and investment in the process.

At this point:

We love even more the possibility of being able to offer interesting materials to children. We believe that we can give children a precious gift by offering the right materials at the right time to enhance children's work and extend their efforts. In order to do this, we realize that we must be atuned to the children by listening.

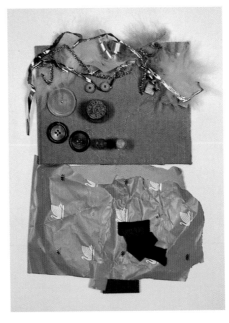

A complete puppet.

Chapter 4

Constructing with Wood Scraps

As the year progresses, new areas of interest and exploration appear. A gift of wood scraps sparks renewed attention to building. Because the teachers know how much children enjoy building in the block area, they decide to collect wood scraps so that the children can make their own three-dimensional structures. The processes of noticing, collecting, sorting, and exploring are called into play once again. It feels like a spiral. Children return to the skills and materials that they have used in the past, and figure out how they might apply those skills in a new and more complex situation.

Familiar problems, such as how to attach and arrange things, present themselves in similar, yet more challenging ways. Each problem is an opportunity for a new area of inquiry. Each problem calls on the children to figure out and attempt possible solutions. Each problem calls on the teacher to support the child's right to have time and space for problem solving.

Two children sort pieces of wood in preparation for our sculpture project.

Odd-shaped scraps become treasures and objects of investigation.

Collecting Scrap Wood

Several months before our actual work with wood scraps, we post a note to parents. We let them know that we will soon be embarking on a project using wood. We ask that they look out for wood scraps. We speak to anyone we know who is a carpenter or who knows a good source for scrap wood.

As boxes of wood scraps come into the classroom, teachers throw out pieces of wood that might cause splinters, and sand very rough parts. We sort scraps into boxes of small, medium, and large shapes, and pick out pieces that would make good bases. This not only tells us what we have, but also what we still need. Children and parents take over this task as they bring in scraps from home.

In particular, we try to collect small scraps of wood in interesting shapes that are not too rough. We also look for any small objects made from wood, such as toothpicks, craft sticks, spools, corks, wood shavings, etc. After all the time and effort collecting and dealing with these wooden pieces, we attempt to develop ways of extending and deepening the constructing experience.

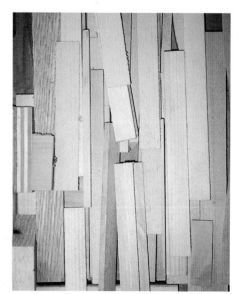

Wood sorted into categories. When similar shapes are placed together, their subtle differences are noticeable. Diamonds, triangles, and trapezoids; big and little rounded forms; squares and rectangles appear as the wood is sorted.

Noticing and sorting

Sorting involves paying attention to the many qualities and characteristics of wood. It is a way to get to know what is available. Sorting wood scraps is an activity that precedes actual building. Children figure out categories for sorting which might be based on shape, size, texture, and color.

"That should go in there because it's straight."
"I'm sorting the long ones."
"These look splintery."

Analytical thinking begins when young children realize that a scribble or shape can become a symbol for something in their world. Being able to break a form down into parts is the basis of analytical thinking. That is what Sean is doing as he names each piece of wood that he finds. The teacher, realizing what is happening, reaches for the clipboard to make sketches and record Sean's descriptions.

While sorting, Sean keeps looking at the different shapes and naming them. He begins to name and study each piece of wood that he picks up.

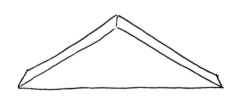

"A different kind of volcano."

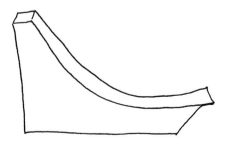

"This looks like a slide."

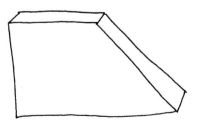

"The back of a garbage truck."

Sanding and Exploring Form

Children and teachers take time to examine the wood scraps, feel their forms, practice sanding with the grain, and sort by size or shape. Sanding is a way of exploring the unique properties of wood. It is a way for children to begin to have an appreciation for the steps necessary to ready a material for use.

We select an assortment of interesting wood shapes to explore. As children arrive in the morning, they are drawn to the materials. Parents also are interested in seeing what the children will do with the materials that they have helped to collect.

As children sand, they are encouraged to practice making constructions. In this way, they come to know the various shapes, the three-dimensional qualities of the shapes, and the potential a shape might hold for building.

Isabella and Sarah spend a long time sanding. Isabella says, "I found a rough place. Where's the sand block?" Sarah responds, "Look what's coming off mine! I'm going to brush the wood dust off of me. How did that wood dust get on me…mine is soft. See what it does when it is very soft? Where's a rough one? Did I sand this?"

"Look, they're friends."

Sarah notices a shape that is exactly like the one she has just finished sanding. She puts the two pieces together and says, "Look, they're friends. One's soft and one's rough, but they look the same."

"I made an airplane."

Sarah experiments with building: "Look, they fit together like this—like a puzzle. Look. I first put one together and I made an airplane."

Constructing with Wood Scraps

In order to prepare for the activity of sanding and building, the teachers purchased sandpaper and tacked and stapled it to blocks of wood that would fit easily into the children's hands.

Other children join the exploration and continue to be motivated by the sandpaper. Kathy notices, "The sandpaper gets light. It gets light because it gets the sand off." Another child says, "This is so rough! My Daddy shaves when he gets up in the morning."

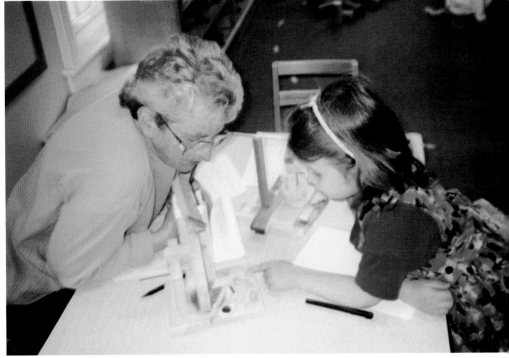

Experimental Building

Taking time for experimental building without the necessity for creating a product gives children a chance to get to know the various shapes and their potential for construction. It also gives children a chance to try out their ideas. The themes that emerge are surprising.

David works through an idea: "I'm trying to make a castle, but I don't know how." (It falls down.)

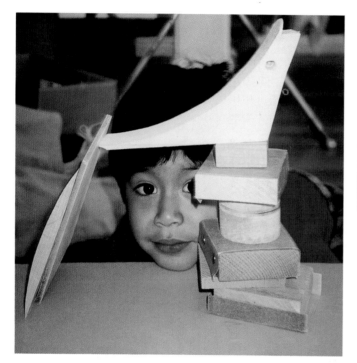

"I was figuring how to make a different kind of castle." (It falls down again.)

"This is a castle and this is a kind of a bridge and this is the top of the bridge, and here is a waterfall."

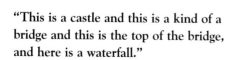

Constructing with Wood Scraps

By keeping track of the interactions and dialogues that occur during this time, a teacher can enable children to revisit their earlier experiences by reading their dialogue out loud. The teacher can also use the children's dialogue to prepare questions to ask on the following day.

Hannah: "That looks like a little house. Let's connect."

Kristi: "Yeah, let's."

Hannah: "This can be the bridge."

Kristi: "This is going to be a tower. Look how tiny this is. This is broken wood."

Hannah: "Lookit here! Here's a dock."

Kristi: "This can be the long wooden…Uh oh, it doesn't fit. It's too long."

Hannah: "I know where we can put that. Right here. No, right here."

Kristi: "This could be the bride's bridge. The bride and her boyfriend are going to be married."

Hannah: "I like this piece because it's thin, and I'm thin, too."

Hannah and Kristi decide to collaborate. The freedom to experiment invites creative and often collaborative solutions.

Thinking in Three Dimensions

A wood construction project can be an introduction to understanding and working with three-dimensional space. Beginning with a few large pieces of wood narrows the focus so that children can expand their exploration of three-dimensional possibilities. "How could I arrange these pieces of wood so that they make a sturdy construction and are interesting to look at from all points of view?" The teacher focuses the interest of the children by posing a question and inviting children to try different arrangements. She turns the arrangement around so children can see it from different directions. Trying more than one solution and exploring possibilities is a way to build flexibility and openness to differing points of view. Looking at something from more than one point of view is a lifelong skill.

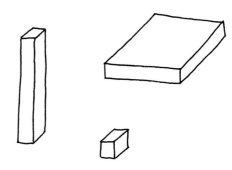

We ask children to choose a few large pieces of wood that they think will make a good base for their constructions.

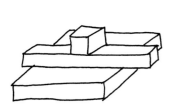

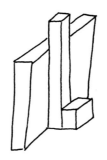

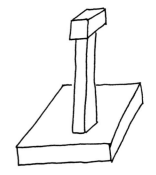

Children try out at least three different ways to arrange their wood scraps. We suggest that they turn their arrangements around and ask themselves, "Is it sturdy? Is it pleasing to look at?" When they are satisfied, they check with a teacher before beginning to use the glue.

A teacher works with a small group of children who are beginning to glue their bases together.

Gluing the base

Determining how much glue to use, how much of the surface to cover, and which surfaces need to be glued is all part of the thinking and constructing process. This stage is where children usually need the most support from adults.

In preparing for gluing, we start with the larger wooden pieces. To avoid confusion, we remove or cover the smaller scraps of wood and save them for another day. Giving children a stopping place—for instance, after they have used five pieces—helps avert disasters. The beginning constructions will be much stronger and ready for additions after they have dried overnight.

Gluing the first pieces is never as simple as it sounds. Here a teacher helps out at a critical moment. Later, when asked how he began his construction, Nicky said, "I put one board on the bottom flat, then I put another on the side, and then hooked it across. First I put a little piece of wood on top of the tall piece." One of the valuable aspects of this experience is that Nicky is aware of and can articulate his own process of thinking while he is constructing.

A parent, noticing children having difficulty with glue bottles, brought brushes and jars into the classroom. Many children prefer these materials.

Children's Advice

While reflecting on the experience with a group of children, a teacher asks, "What advice do you think we should give to the children in the other class before they start to glue?" With the teacher's help, the children make a sign for the glueing area:

"Use the brush kind."
"Glue at the bottom and then at the top."
"Glue up, down, sideways to sideways."
"Get a friend to help you hold the pieces together and count to ten."
"Put the glue in the right place."
"Glue it in two places."
"Watch the glue."
"Don't hold it (the glue bottle) up in the air."
"To have the teeniest piece on the bottom doesn't work."

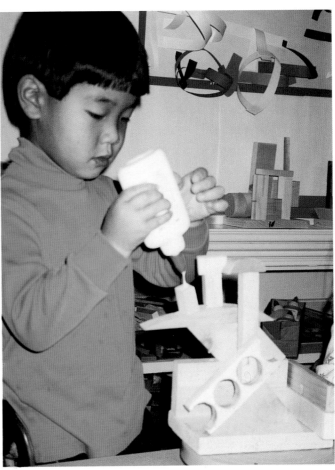

A turntable allows Nicholas to turn his structure around as he adds additional pieces. It encourages more three-dimensional work and more three-dimensional thinking.

The first day of gluing is definitely the most difficult. It is a good day for a parent to help out. Alex notices a few rough places and gets sanding blocks to smooth them out.

Expanding Three-Dimensional Thinking

Letting constructions dry overnight before continuing allows the sculptures to harden. It also allows children to step back from their work, think about it overnight, and return with new enthusiasm and new ideas. Children are delighted to discover that their constructions are much sturdier and stronger once they have dried. They can pick them up, turn them over, and generally have a look at what they remember doing on the previous day.

Once the initial structure has hardened, it is easy to add additional pieces. Remind children to try each piece in several different places before gluing. Encourage them to turn their constructions around every now and then so they can look at them from different points of view.

Max tries placing a piece high up on his construction.

Next, Max tries placing the piece low, near the bottom of the construction.

Max turns his sculpture around and is pleased to notice how different his construction looks from this point of view. He sees a part of his construction that he did not see before. When Max looks at his sculpture from a different point of view, he sees it anew. The process is similar to rereading a paper or a book. Each time that you read it, you think about it a little differently.

Thinking about Space

Space, or negative shape, is an important part of any construction. Figuring out how to construct a place to look through the construction is often a problem. Usually, one or two children in the class will create some sort of "see-through" place, perhaps a bridge or door or house. They can share their construction strategies. Creating a see-through place is a way of making the construction process more complex and interesting.

"I glued this piece on, but it fell down and made a triangle."

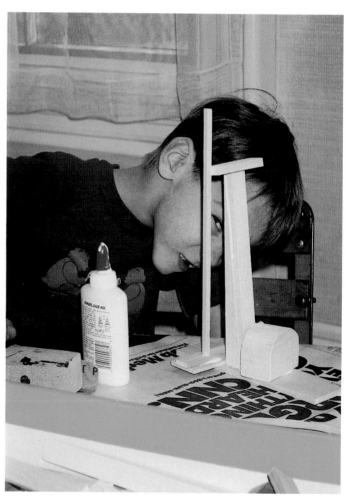

David returns to his construction and adds more pieces on the following day. As his construction grows higher, a teacher might ask him if he intends to make it wider as well.

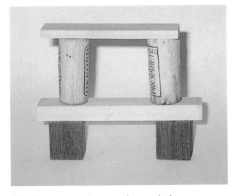

Finding two pieces of wood that are the same height and topping them with another is one way to create a doorway or opening.

Discussing solutions to the problem of how to build a bridge or doorway can help a group of children expand their ideas and options. Sometimes, the nature of the materials can foster problem solving. Making some smaller pieces of wood available, especially pieces that are the same length, could help at this point. Our collection of corks comes in handy!

Miriam looks through the rectangular negative shape in her house construction.

Constructions and Stories Grow More Complex

Children often name and talk about their constructions as they work. Sometimes, the shape of a wooden scrap fuels an idea. At other times, an idea prompts a child to search for wood of a particular shape and size.

A clipboard makes it easier to record the children's thoughts before they are lost. Displaying children's words alongside the constructions helps adults understand how children think.

"This is an antique airplane with a decoration on the back…This is an explore spaceship and it explores in the night."

"I just wanted to build a design. This stick is a little bridge because this is a house for bugs. This is a bridge for bugs."

"You know why I wanted to do this? Because it made me think of a boat."

"What gave me the idea? I like long things and round things. It's like a building."

"This is a house for my animal, so I'm experimenting with different points of view."

Julianna explains, "I was thinking this was a helicopter above a dock with a boat going through the water. This is another part of a helicopter. It's spinning around like helicopters do. Half of it is behind the clouds...I'm an artist and I practice pretty much the whole day when my brother falls asleep."

(Right) Julianna watches with pleasure as the teacher sketches her construction. The teacher plans to share this story with Julianna's parents, and the sketch will help her remember.

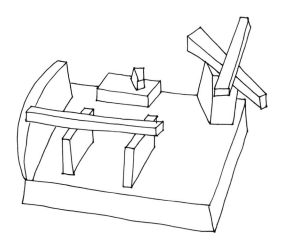

Teacher's sketch of Julianna's sculpture.

Julianna's sketch of her completed sculpture.

Children begin to look at the materials in new ways, thinking about how they might incorporate them into their own or a friend's construction. Small wooden objects can encourage children to add details to their constructions.

Renewing the Project

As children complete one step and are ready for another, bringing out shapes that are different becomes a new catalyst. Medium shapes and small shapes might be brought out on different days. They can be used both to make a structure more interesting and sturdier.

Sean works on his construction for the third time.

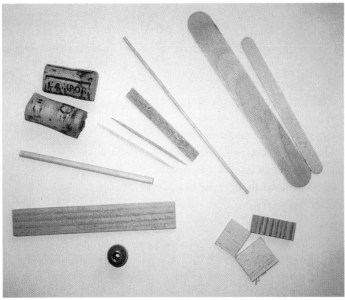

When you start looking, you will notice that there are many everyday materials made from wood.

Tongue depressors, craft sticks, and wooden applicators are materials teachers often have available, and they are excellent motivators for additional work. Collections of spiral wood shavings, bark, twigs, and corks are also materials that can be brought out on different days. Another possibility is to ask children to make a plan for what they would like to add next. "If you wanted to construct something such as a ladder, a ramp, or a propeller, how could you do it?"

When we think back to Sean's initial encounters with wooden shapes, we see that they set the stage for more involved work. Sean went on to use the triangle that he sanded in his construction.

What We Learned...

About processes:

In the common experience of constructing with wood scraps, we discovered so many opportunities for learning three-dimensional concepts. For instance, only in the last few years did we, as teachers, pay attention to the powerful areas of inquiry that sanding a shape or experimental building could provoke. Recording children's conversations opened up this avenue of learning for us. Now we give more space and attention to both of these processes.

About learning:

Actually, each part of the wood construction experience—working with balance, points of view, nega-tive space, gluing—has led to more in-depth learning experiences for both teachers and children. And, as the children's investment grew, so did the interest and involvement of the parents. Teachers and parents became even more aware of the complexity involved in working with such apparently simple materials.

At this point:

This chapter shows how rich an experience can be if allowed space, time, and support.

A grandparent visits the classroom and helps out by recording the children's explanations. In the process, she gets to know her grandchild and other children in a deeper way.

Chapter 5

Extending and Displaying Our Work

few children start looking through the boxes of found objects on the shelf and begin arranging the objects on their wood constructions. Suddenly, the objects are transformed into vehicles, magic balls, people, lights, and flag poles. The teachers ask those children to show their ideas to the rest of the class. The other children like the ideas very much, and begin to return to the studio to retrieve their constructions and continue their work.

Children make a game of placing some of the beautiful materials on their wood constructions.

New Avenues of Discovery

In order to help children make thoughtful choices about materials and placement, we look for a way to channel and build on their enthusiasm. We decide to help them see the differences in value and hue within one color. Sorting objects by color gives us a new focus, and builds on the children's earlier interest.

"Choose one color and collect objects only of that color. Notice that even one color has many variations. If your color is purple, find some light purple objects and some dark purple objects. Perhaps you will even find some violet objects that sparkle or are transparent." As soon as we limit children to one color, the possibilities open up. Children become much keener and more discriminating observers—and so do the teachers. Discussions focus on whether a certain object is in the color range.

Children and teachers together made this color wheel from found objects.

Children help one another gather and evaluate their objects. As they add color objects to their sculptures, the children remember the suggestion of trying an object in several places. Because constructions at this point generally reach into space, many opportunities for exploring high and low places, and for looking from different points of view keep presenting themselves. To support children's explorations, we once again keep the glue out of reach until the children decide on the arrangement they like best.

Anya tries out different ways to arrange her purple objects. We notice her purple shirt and discuss the idea that many children have strong color preferences.

More Three-Dimensional Problem Solving

Gluing problems crop up once again, and children have to find still more solutions. They refer to their list of gluing ideas. Beads and round objects present special problems.

Stepping back to look and take pleasure in what you have done is also part of the learning process. This could be a time to listen to one another's stories and to celebrate together.

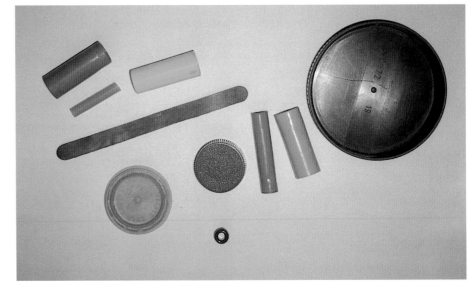

A collection of blue objects.

If children want to glue an object to the side of a wood construction, they learn that they have to hold it for a few minutes, or that they need to turn the sculpture on its side.

Child and teacher revisit the process together: "Mine is called a shooter and I pretend it says, 'Watch out for the shooters you have.' Shooters should have very many spaces. That's why I put in lots of spaces."

"It has some beautiful parts that are wood. It has some beautiful parts that are blue. I really love it."

Drawing the Constructions

We become interested in the way children move from one language to another in the Reggio Emilia approach. In particular, we notice that teachers often encourage children to draw their constructions, so we decide to see if our four- and five-year-old students can draw their intricate constructions. We reason that the handling and constructing must influence children's drawing. However, we haven't tried observational drawing yet with this group of children.

This exploration takes place in the spring, so many but not all of the children can, at this point, draw basic shapes. Although skeptical, we ask children to choose the point of view of their sculpture that they like best and try to draw it. We give them black fine-tipped markers and white paper. We say, "Consider how the overall shape of your construction will best fit onto your paper."

Elie prepares his eyes and hands for drawing. By sketching first with his finger, or with a closed marker, he trains himself to translate the relative sizes and shapes of the objects into the language of line. He also develops an intuitive understanding of how and where to place one object in relation to another. Elie is training himself to refer to his construction in order to figure out his next step.

Preparing for drawing

We tell children that this is a difficult task, but to try it. Before each child begins, and before giving out the fine-tipped markers, we spend a few minutes looking. We ask each child to point out the shape with which they plan to begin, and to draw the shape with a finger first for practice. Once they do that, we give them a marker.

During the act of drawing, a child sees his understandings and abilities grow step by step. First, Zachary draws his entire structure with the fine-tipped marker and writes his name. Then, to color the objects, he chooses the colors of markers that match the objects on his sculpture.

Amazing Drawings

We are amazed by the results of this experiment! We didn't know that children this age could draw so well from observation. This differs from drawing the collage people because, in this case, we are asking children to draw objects that present perplexing problems of perspective. These are problems some of the adults don't feel they can handle. The children are simply open to trying, and the pleasure at their achievements is obvious. As teachers we learn that, although some children cannot yet write their names, they can draw their constructions!

A month of experiences that involved handling, selecting shapes, sanding, positioning, gluing, and experimenting with points of view all seem to come together as children recall the process of building their constructions.

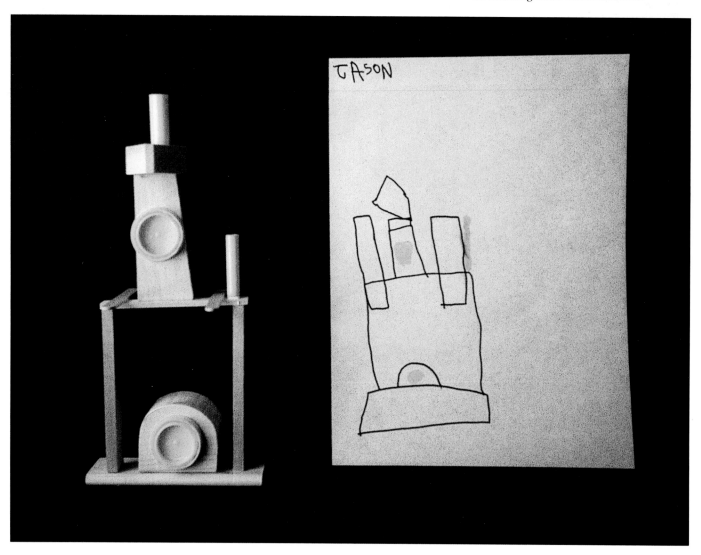

One child is deeply involved in his drawing and creates a scene around his wood sculpture.

Some children only draw one or two shapes. For those children, that is a major achievement. Many draw surprisingly sophisticated renditions of their constructions. Some go on to try drawing their sculptures from several points of view. Drawing sculptures is a way of remembering and thinking about the problems, solutions, and accomplishments of this project. It is a way of revisiting the considerations involved in building something three-dimensional and complex.

In looking over the final results with a group of children, an adult visitor asks, "If my grandson wanted to build something like this, what should I tell him?" The child replies, "If I brought my picture, I could remember how to do it to tell your grandchild how to do it." The child's drawing has become a map for thinking.

A Way of Thinking

We think back to the beginning of this experience and realize that bringing materials into the classroom and discovering their potential for learning involves many of the same process skills used in math and science and interpreting literature. It's a way of thinking about things. It helps both teachers and children become more aware of how they think. The experience also refines our aesthetic sensibilities, and gives both adults and children a framework for learning life skills.

Thomas points out the three pieces that formed the base of his construction.

He discusses the evolution of his ideas, "It was a boat, like a marina. I think I'm showing her the thing standing up. It's like an antenna. The two green things are like guns. There was something I could shoot out of the big one. It was so cool."

As we go along, we realize, once again, the need to tell our story. Thomas helps us select photographs that explain the process he went through and the insights he had while building his wood construction. These photos show Thomas thinking and remembering.

Extending and Displaying Our Work

The need to tell our story

Telling our story is a way of documenting our experience. The process of documenting helps us understand the children's thinking processes, their desires, and the surprises that they have lived through. Documenting gives teachers an opportunity to re-examine why they think a particular experience is important. It also gives them a chance to think about what they might do differently in the future.

We combine the photos with transcriptions of our notes and recordings to tell, in the words of the children and the teachers, the many ways of thinking and the kinds of problems that we solved during our journey with materials.

Documenting is a vehicle for communication between teachers and between teachers and children. It is also a vehicle for communicating with parents. Parents become stronger participants in the life of the classroom when they can follow the interesting work that is taking place. When children's words and images are placed next to their work, parents become much more interested and stay longer in the classroom.

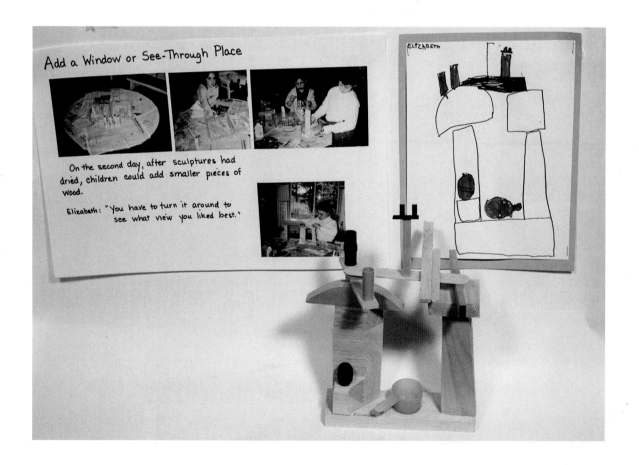

Add a Window or See-Through Place

On the second day, after sculptures had dried, children could add smaller pieces of wood.

Elizabeth: "You have to turn it around to see what view you liked best."

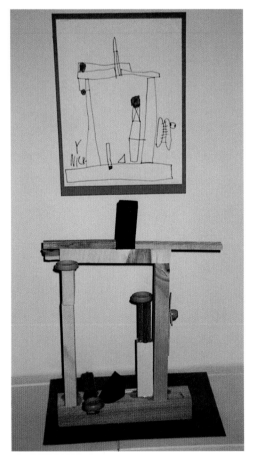

Nicky's Story

"It was difficult to draw the top part—the part that sticks out—because I couldn't really see how it was made."

We think a lot about Nicky's comments. We feel that his words indicate that he had become aware of the difficulties involved in moving from construction to the new medium of drawing. Rita comments that Nicky is primarily interested in the outline or the shape of things. She recalls that "he never cared much about color or detail. What he wanted was the overall shape, so he would have been working very hard to get the contour. I watched him all year long and was fascinated by his work."

Day One

Day Three

Day Four

"I just didn't know with my eyes how long it was."

Day Five

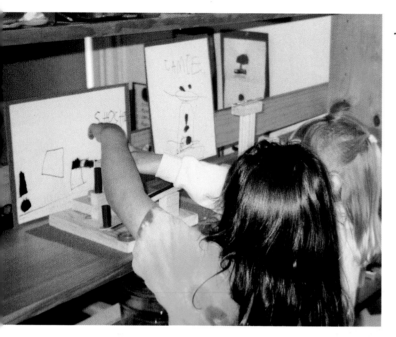

Displaying to Communicate

We are eager to set up the children's work and see it from a distance. When we arrive at an attractive arrangement, we feel that we communicate our respect for the children and for their achievements.

These children look at their work and realize how much they have done and how much progress they have made.

Shoshi enjoys looking at her construction and notices big differences in the lightness and darkness of the purple objects that she used.

Extending and Displaying Our Work

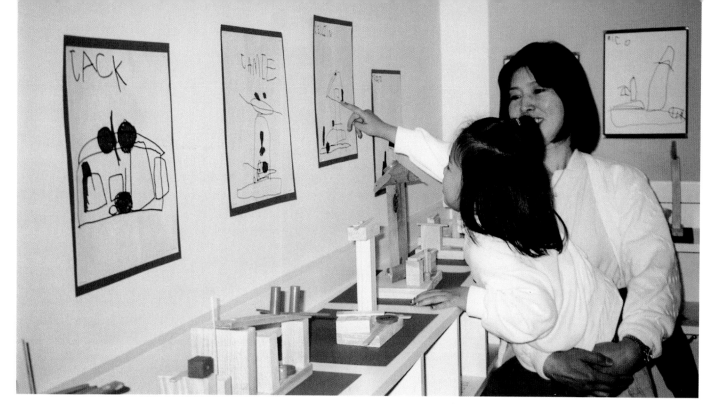

As constructions are completed, the teachers move them into the hallway to a more public place. By arranging an aesthetic display with care, we show our respect for the children's work. The children feel a great sense of pride and accomplishment. By displaying, we make it possible for the children themselves to communicate their pleasure and achievements to family and friends.

For all the adults who enter the school, the displays are strong statements about children's potential.

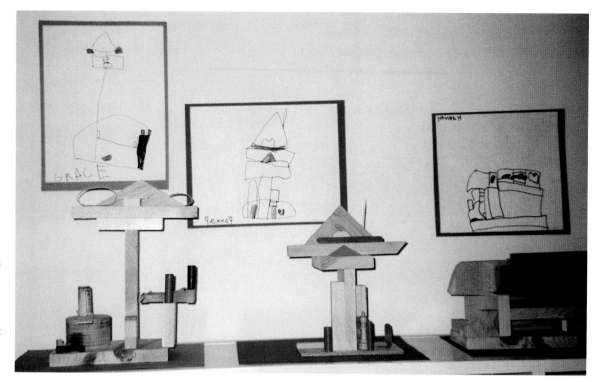

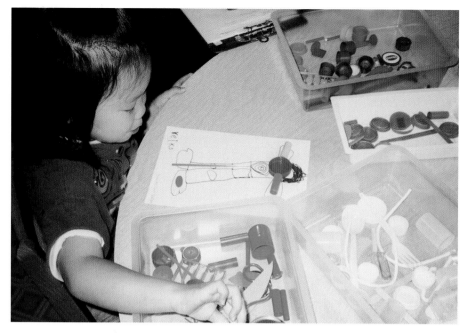

Using her drawing as a blueprint, this child thinks again about the parts of her body and uses materials symbolically.

"Here's just the thing. This could be a leg. This could be a foot! Green is a good color for me."

The Journey Continues...

Parents respond with interest to the display. They look at other children's work, not only the work of their own child. They become more interested in the kinds of interactions between children and between children and materials that they see documented in the children's creations, photos, and dialogues. This is a way to begin to create a sense of community in the classroom. We feel that we are beginning to understand what it means to see potential in materials. We are amazed by the many ways in which we can use materials.

The teacher helps by using a glue gun to attach the objects to a sheet of clear acetate.

Displaying this child's two self-portraits along with photographs of the process incites the curiosity of the other children in the room, and gives clues about possible ways of representing oneself with materials.

What We Learned...

About documentation:

As we reviewed children's work and listened to their reflections, we noticed that the documentation process helped us to know the children and their learning styles in very profound ways. We kept notebooks handy so that we could record children's thoughts and conversations. Tape recordings helped us to go back and find direct quotes and sequence moments of understanding. Photographs and videos were great ways of sharing our experiences with parents and validating the children's efforts. They were also ways to help children reflect.

About drawing:

We found that drawing from the constructions, or moving from one language of expression to another, is a powerful learning and documenting tool. The most effective way we know to support children as they draw is to try the same thing you are asking of them.

At this point:

To help us think back over the children's work that we have witnessed, we posed a series of open-ended questions to ourselves and to parents:

- What does it mean to children when they have sought out, discovered, and collected materials themselves?
- Does this affect the way they use and care for those materials?
- Are they more thoughtful, focused, and pleased with their efforts when they have been engaged in the process right from the beginning?

We invite you to try working with unusual materials and to study what happens—what is meaningful. We are eager to continue the next phase of our journey!

Resources for the Reggio Emilia Approach

The Hundred Languages of Children, The Reggio Emilia Approach—Advanced Reflections, second edition, edited by Carolyn Edwards, Lella Gandini, and George Forman. Greenwich, CT: Ablex Publishing Corp., 1998.

Louise Boyd Cadwell, *Bringing Reggio Emilia Home: An Innovative Approach to Early Childhood Education.* New York: Teachers College Press, 1997.

Roda Kellogg, *Analyzing Children's Art.* Mountain View, CA: Mayfield Publishing Co., 1970.

Information about the Reggio Emilia approach published by the city of Reggio Emilia, Italy, is distributed in the United States by Reggio Children/USA. A packet including a bibliography of books, articles, slides, videos, and drawings by children is available by writing to:

Reggio Children/USA
2460 16th Street NW
Washington, DC 20009
(202) 265-9090
fax: (202) 265-9161